Original title:
The Road to Healing

Copyright © 2024 Swan Charm
All rights reserved.

Author: Liisi Lendorav
ISBN HARDBACK: 978-9916-89-979-3
ISBN PAPERBACK: 978-9916-89-980-9
ISBN EBOOK: 978-9916-89-981-6

Grace Unfolding

In the stillness of dawn, grace does appear,
Soft whispers of love, drawing us near.
Each step on the path, a blessing bestowed,
In every small moment, His presence flowed.

Hearts open wide, like petals in bloom,
Sheltered by faith, dispelling all gloom.
With hands lifted high, we search for the light,
In the depths of our sorrow, there is pure sight.

Crumbs of Comfort

In the chaos of life, crumbs fall from above,
Tiny morsels of mercy, reminders of love.
Each trial we face, a chance to receive,
The sweetness of solace, if we just believe.

Gathering hope like treasures so dear,
In the midst of despair, we cast off our fear.
For even the smallest of gifts can ignite,
A flame of compassion, in the heart's quiet night.

The Embrace of Serenity

In the hush of the evening, peace gently flows,
Wrapped in His arms, where true comfort grows.
With each breath we take, still waters we find,
A haven of quiet, for the restless mind.

Beneath a starry sky, our worries retract,
In the embrace of serenity, we are intact.
Trusting the journey, we walk hand in hand,
Faithful in spirit, united we stand.

Tides of Transformation

As the waves of grace wash over our shore,
We rise with the tide, renewed evermore.
In the cycle of life, we dance and we sway,
Embracing change, in His light we stay.

Each challenge a chance, a season to grow,
With roots ever deep, through the storms we know.
In love's gentle calling, we find our true place,
Lost in the beauty of infinite grace.

Pathways to the Divine

In quiet woods, we seek the light,
Soft whispers guide the weary night.
Each step unfolds the sacred road,
With open hearts, we share this load.

The sunlit dawn reveals the way,
With faith, we step, come what may.
Through trials dark, the spirits rise,
In love we find, the truest prize.

From mountain high to valley deep,
In every breath, our souls we keep.
The journey's truth, a gentle sign,
In every heart, resides the divine.

In Search of Wholeness

A broken heart, a fractured soul,
In search of peace, we seek the whole.
With every prayer, we rise anew,
Embracing light that shines so true.

Through trials faced, the shadows creep,
Yet in the dark, our promise weep.
A bond unbroken, love's embrace,
In unity, we find our place.

Oh sacred paths we tread with care,
In giving thanks, we do our share.
For wholeness found, in every part,
Is stitched together, thread by heart.

Blossoms of Renewal

In sacred ground, new flowers bloom,
Each petal whispers, banishing gloom.
A sign of hope, in colors bright,
From darkest nights, emerges light.

The cycle turns, as seasons blend,
From winter's chill, new warmth ascend.
In every bud, a promise glows,
That life returns, as nature knows.

With gentle winds, the spirits sway,
In harmony, they dance and play.
Renewal's touch, a grace divine,
In every heart, sweet love entwines.

Reflections in the Heart's Mirror

In quiet moments, truth reveals,
The heart's soft whispers, gently heals.
A gaze within, the soul laid bare,
In stillness found, love's tender care.

Reflections dance in sacred light,
Each shadow traced, a guiding sight.
With every tear, a lesson learned,
In every joy, our hearts have turned.

A mirror holds the depths we seek,
In every silence, wisdom speaks.
With open hearts, we find our way,
In love's embrace, forever stay.

Where Faith Meets Forgiveness

In the stillness of the night,
Hearts seek the path of grace.
Whispers of mercy take flight,
Embracing our broken place.

With each prayer, burdens released,
Love's embrace, a gentle tide.
In our weakness, strength increased,
Faith walks with us as our guide.

Forgiveness flows like a river,
Washing sins, making us whole.
In the light, we shall consider,
Renewed spirits, pure and goal.

Through trials, we learn to see,
Each moment a chance to mend.
Together in unity,
Where faith and love transcends.

With open hearts, we ascend,
Rising above pain and doubt.
In unity, our souls blend,
In forgiveness, love's true route.

From Darkness Into Light

In shadows deep, hope does dwell,
A flicker ignites the soul's fight.
Through stormy seas, we hear the bell,
Calling us from darkness to light.

Each step taken, a whisper of grace,
Guiding us through uncertain night.
In every heart, a sacred space,
Where shadows yield to purest light.

With faith's lantern, we find our way,
Through the valleys, rugged and steep.
In trials faced, we shall not stray,
For His promise, our hearts will keep.

As dawn breaks, the world awakes,
Each moment, a blessing bestowed.
In the warmth of love, our hearts ache,
To share the light on life's road.

Together we rise, hand in hand,
From the depths of despair, we climb.
In unity, we make our stand,
From darkness into light, we shine.

The Sacred Steps of Renewal

Upon the path of grace we walk,
Each step a pledge to start anew.
In silence, hear the whispers talk,
Revealing love in every hue.

Through trials faced, we grow in worth,
Building bridges, hearts align.
In every moment, a rebirth,
Your spirit in my spirit, shine.

The sacred dance of life unfolds,
Each turn revealing truth untold.
With faith, the heart's warmth enfolds,
Creating bonds, like threads of gold.

As seasons change, so do our souls,
From winter's grasp to spring's embrace.
In the journey, the spirit rolls,
Finding joy in every place.

Together we rise, gather the light,
With open hearts, the journey flows.
Each sacred step brings new insight,
In renewal, love's garden grows.

A Sanctuary of Solace

In the hush of the sacred space,
Where dreams mend and tears are dried.
In the warmth of a soft embrace,
We find peace where love resides.

The heart's refuge, calm and still,
Whispered prayers ascend like smoke.
In every moment, grace we instill,
In solitude, we dare to hope.

With every breath, a soft release,
In silence, the spirit unfolds.
Here in this place, we find our peace,
As the sacred story is told.

Together, we share this light,
In the stillness, hearts align.
A sanctuary to honor the fight,
Where our souls in unity twine.

Under stars that watch above,
In this haven, fear takes flight.
With open arms, we foster love,
A sanctuary of pure delight.

New Dawn of Understanding

In the silence of the night, we pray,
Seeking wisdom to light our way.
Hearts open wide, we humbly stand,
Guided gently by His hand.

Each thought a seed of grace we sow,
Through trials faced, our spirits grow.
United in faith, we find our song,
Together we rise, together we belong.

Beneath the veil of morning light,
New insights bloom, a wondrous sight.
In shared reflections, truth appears,
A gift bestowed to calm our fears.

With every dawn, a chance to learn,
As embers glow, our hearts still burn.
To seek not answers, but the quest,
In humble awe, we find our rest.

Oh luminous grace, in us reside,
In the depths of love, we take our stride.
With open hearts and hands outstretched,
In every moment, we are blessed.

Spirit's Voyage

On waves of faith, our spirits soar,
In trust, we sail to distant shore.
Through storms and calm, we find our peace,
With every breath, our doubts released.

The winds of change, both fierce and fair,
Carry our hopes in sacred air.
With stars as guides, we navigate,
A journey mapped by love's own fate.

In whispered prayers, we share our dreams,
Each drop of grace, a flowing stream.
Across the seas, our souls entwine,
A tapestry of the divine.

Every sunset marks a sacred space,
A moment rich with love and grace.
Together we wander, side by side,
In Spirit's arms, we safely glide.

Beyond the horizon, where peace awaits,
We find our rest at heaven's gates.
With hearts aligned, we journey on,
Awakening to a brighter dawn.

Compassion's Journey

In every gaze, a story told,
In tender hearts, compassion unfolds.
With open arms, we share the load,
In kindness' light, we find our road.

Each step we take, a chance to heal,
With gentle words, our truth reveal.
For every soul that feels alone,
In love's embrace, they find a home.

Through laughter shared and sorrows borne,
We stitch the seams of lives reborn.
In every act, a seed is sown,
Compassion's bloom, our hearts have grown.

As rivers flow to join the sea,
So too, we weave our unity.
In every hand, a promise shines,
To guide us through the toughest times.

With every sunset, we reflect,
The lives we've touched, the love we've shaped.
In compassion's light, we shall unite,
Together as one, in shared delight.

Guiding Stars of Hope

In the darkness, bright they shine,
Each a whisper, divine and fine.
They guide the lost with gentle light,
Leading hearts through the night.

With every twinkle, dreams take flight,
Promises held in celestial height.
A compass made of radiant grace,
Lighting the path we embrace.

When storms arise and shadows fall,
These guiding stars, they heed our call.
Through trials faced and fears exposed,
Their heavenly glow ever disclosed.

From ages past, their wisdom flows,
In quiet moments, the spirit knows.
Hope's embrace, a soothing balm,
In sacred trust, our souls find calm.

As we journey, hand in hand,
The stars remind us, we will stand.
In unity, with hearts aligned,
For love's deep light, we're intertwined.

Fountains of Mercy

From heights above, the waters pour,
Washing over a weary shore.
Renewing souls with gentle grace,
Fountains of mercy, our sacred space.

In every drop, compassion flows,
Healing the wounds that life bestows.
The thirsty hearts shall find their fill,
In the depths of love, our spirits still.

As rivers merge and join the sea,
Together, we find unity.
With every blessing, love we share,
Fountains of mercy, beyond compare.

Let gratitude spring forth like rain,
In every heart, erase the pain.
A cycle pure, our lives renew,
In the embrace of the utmost true.

So may we drink from this sacred well,
Where stories of love and grace do dwell.
In every moment, let kindness flow,
Fountains of mercy, forever grow.

A Symphony of Rest

In quiet moments, peace shall rise,
A symphony beneath the skies.
Notes of solace fill the air,
In gentle whispers of prayer.

Each breath a melody of grace,
In soft embrace, we find our place.
The world's clamor fades away,
In stillness, our hearts learn to sway.

With every heartbeat, calm is found,
In sacred spaces, joy unbound.
The harmonies of love resound,
A symphony in silence crowned.

Beneath the stars, we lay our cares,
In trust and faith, a world that shares.
A lullaby of hope and rest,
In every moment, we are blessed.

So close your eyes, let worries cease,
In this symphony, find your peace.
For in these notes, the heart will see,
The restful joy of simply being free.

The Quietude of Faith

In quietude, our spirits rise,
With gentle whispers, faith defies.
The burden lightens, fears depart,
In sacred stillness, we find our heart.

Through trials faced and doubts confessed,
In silent trust, we are truly blessed.
An anchor strong when storms abound,
A refuge safe, where hope is found.

In moments hushed, the soul can hear,
The tender voice that draws us near.
With every prayer, the bond grows tight,
Illuminating paths with holy light.

As nature breathes, we breathe in time,
Encircled by the love divine.
With every heartbeat, faith embarks,
Guiding us like the brightest sparks.

So let us dwell in this embrace,
In quietude, we find our grace.
With hearts aligned, forever true,
The quietude of faith, anew.

Tides of Renewal

In the dawn light, hope arises,
Waves of grace wash over the shore,
Hearts once weary, now revitalized,
With every tide, we seek for more.

Nature whispers soft and clear,
The promise of new beginnings shines,
As the sun paints the sky sincere,
We embrace the love that intertwines.

Every moment holds a chance,
To shed the burdens of the past,
With faith, we join in grateful dance,
And trust that joy will ever last.

The earth sings sweet redemption's song,
Reminding us to let things flow,
In each heartbeat, we belong,
To the cycles we are meant to know.

So let the tides of change befriend,
Our souls in constant, gentle fight,
With every wave, may we ascend,
In the warmth of divine light.

In Pursuit of Peace

In silence deep, our spirits yearn,
For the whisper of love divine,
As each candle flickers and burns,
We seek a truth in heart and mind.

Mountains tall, they stand so proud,
Yet valleys low hold comfort still,
In skies where prayers are echoed loud,
We journey forth with steadfast will.

As waters flow through ancient rocks,
May we learn to bend and sway,
In patience, love unlocks the box,
To guide our hearts along the way.

In every step, the light draws near,
With every breath, we find a way,
In trials faced, we shall not fear,
For peace shall bloom in hearts today.

So let us walk this sacred path,
With open hearts and hands embraced,
In pursuit of peace, we feel the swath,
Of grace that weaves in every space.

Beneath the Shelter of Wings

In shadows deep, we seek a home,
A haven warm where love is found,
Beneath the wings of grace, we roam,
In refuge safe on holy ground.

The storms may rage and winds may blow,
Yet here within, we find our rest,
With every tear, the spirit flows,
In trust that we are truly blessed.

The gentle touch of mercy's hand,
Wraps around our fragile hearts,
In every struggle, we understand,
Our faith in love will not depart.

In unity, let voices rise,
With hymns of hope that fill the air,
For under wings, the soul complies,
To lift our burdens with the prayer.

So let us gather, hearts in tune,
In spirit bound, through thick and thin,
Within the shelter, we are strewn,
In love's embrace, we find our kin.

Streams of Forgiveness

Like rivers flowing to the sea,
Forgiveness pours from heart to heart,
In every soul, a chance to be,
Released from chains that tear apart.

Each drop a grace, a gentle sigh,
Washing away the pain we hold,
In tears we weave, we learn to fly,
Transforming wounds to stories told.

In every challenge, there's a way,
To let the past dissolve in light,
In echoes soft, we hear the say,
Love conquers darkness, brings forth bright.

So let us gather by the streams,
With open hearts, we share our pain,
In unity, we weave our dreams,
A tapestry where love will reign.

With faith, may we embrace the flow,
In all our journeys, big and small,
For in forgiveness, we shall grow,
United in the sacred call.

From Ashes to Blessings

From ashes rise, the spirit sings,
Renewed by grace, as hope takes wing.
In trials faced, our hearts ignite,
With faith as our guide, we find the light.

The past may bind, yet love breaks chains,
In every loss, a lesson gains.
Through sacred hands, we mend and heal,
From brokenness, new truths reveal.

A gentle breeze, the whisper calls,
In quietude, the spirit sprawls.
Embrace the dawn, let shadows flee,
From ashes born, we live to be.

In every tear, a seed will grow,
Through darkest nights, the blessings flow.
Our journey twists, but faith remains,
From ashes strong, the heart sustains.

Lanterns Through the Dark

In shadows deep, a lantern glows,
With every flame, the spirit knows.
Through darkened paths, we seek the light,
In unity, the heart takes flight.

The guiding stars above us beam,
Their brilliance paints the night-time dream.
With whispers soft, they call us near,
In faith, we find the path so clear.

Each step we take, a promise grows,
Through trials faced, the courage flows.
In moments still, our hearts shall sing,
For every night, the dawn will bring.

With every lantern, shadows flee,
In every soul, a symphony.
Together we walk, hand in hand,
Through darkened nights, we understand.

Heartstrings of Compassion

In gentle hands, compassion lies,
With every act, the heart complies.
A simple smile, a kind embrace,
In love we find our sacred space.

With open hearts, we share our tears,
Together brave, we face our fears.
For every sorrow, joy remains,
In shared burdens, the spirit gains.

The threads that bind us, strong and true,
Create a tapestry anew.
In every step, we rise, we fall,
Through heartstrings pulled, we heed the call.

In warmth and grace, we lift each other,
For every soul, a cherished brother.
Through selfless acts, the world shall see,
In heartstrings tied, we all are free.

The Divinity Within

In every breath, the sacred dwells,
A quiet voice, that softly tells.
Through trials faced, we seek the spark,
In darkness deep, we find our mark.

With every thought, a prayer ascends,
In hearts aligned, divinity bends.
We rise as one, through love's embrace,
In unity, we find our place.

The light within, a guiding flame,
Through every challenge, peace we claim.
In stillness found, the spirit soars,
A sacred bond that ever pours.

Together we walk this winding road,
In kindness shared, our spirits load.
The divinity, in each heartbeat,
In every soul, love is complete.

Steps Toward Redemption

In shadows deep, we seek the light,
A path of faith, through darkest night.
Each humble step, our spirits rise,
In silent prayer, our hearts comprise.

Forgiveness flows, like rivers wide,
Washing away all pain inside.
With open hands, we lift our plea,
To find the hope that sets us free.

The narrow road, though steep and long,
Is paved with grace, our spirits strong.
We journey forth with steadfast trust,
In every trial, we find our just.

Embracing change, we shed the past,
In every moment, healing lasts.
United hearts, we walk as one,
A melody of love begun.

So take the step, though fears may bind,
In search of peace, true joy we find.
Each breath we take, a sacred chance,
To dance in faith, our souls' romance.

Whispers of Divine Comfort

In quiet moments, hear the call,
A soft embrace, through trials small.
The gentle breeze, a soothing balm,
In whispered words, our hearts find calm.

Amidst the storms, we find our way,
With faith as bright as dawn's first ray.
In shadows cast, the light will break,
A promise made, for love's sweet sake.

Each tear we shed, a sacred stream,
A path to peace, a sacred dream.
In every doubt, His hand we trace,
We rise anew, in boundless grace.

With open hearts, we seek the truth,
In childlike trust, we find our youth.
The whispers soft, like lullabies,
Remind us of the skies' blue ties.

So, resting deep in faith's embrace,
We find our home, our sacred space.
In love's sweet hold, we stand as one,
A journey blessed, 'til day is done.

Ascending from Ashes

From ashes cold, we rise anew,
In faith's embrace, a vision true.
With every flame, our spirits soar,
In trials faced, we find the door.

The burden of the past grows light,
As dawn unveils the coming light.
From grief's great weight, our hearts align,
In trust we find, His love divine.

Each step we take, a sacred start,
To mend the wounds within the heart.
In unity, we break the chains,
In freedom found, true love remains.

The road ahead, though fraught with fears,
Is paved with hope, and softened tears.
We walk as one, through fire and rain,
Transformed by grace, we'll rise again.

So let the ashes fall away,
In love's embrace, we'll find our way.
With open souls, we greet the day,
And trust the light to guide our stay.

The Journey of Grace

In every heart, a story waits,
A path of love that never hesitates.
With every step, we learn to see,
The grace that flows, eternally.

Through valleys low and mountains grand,
We hold His promise, hand in hand.
In joy and sorrow, we redefine,
A tapestry of love divine.

Each lesson learned, a gentle guide,
In faith we trust, through every stride.
The journey's worth, though fraught with pain,
In every loss, there's much to gain.

With open hearts, we seek the truth,
In every moment, reclaim our youth.
In laughter shared, in tears embraced,
We find the strength that love has placed.

So let us walk this sacred quest,
With spirits driven, we are blessed.
In every breath, His love we trace,
We rise together, the journey of grace.

The Quiet Convalescence

In stillness I await Your grace,
A gentle touch, a warm embrace.
Wounds of spirit, slowly mend,
With faith as guide and love to tend.

The whispers of the morning light,
Bring solace to the endless night.
With every breath, I feel You near,
In this retreat, I cast my fear.

The quiet waters flow so deep,
In peace I stand, in You I leap.
Your healing balm, a soft caress,
In silence, Lord, I find my rest.

Hope renewed like dawn's first ray,
In every heart, You find a way.
With gratitude, I rise anew,
In love's embrace, I dwell in You.

A Divine Compass

In shadows cast, I seek Your light,
A guiding star through darkest night.
Your whispers lead, a soft refrain,
In faith, I travel through the pain.

When tempests roar and doubts arise,
Your words of comfort are my skies.
Each turn I take, a sacred path,
Within Your love, I find the math.

Through winding roads and hidden trails,
Your presence with me never fails.
With heart aflame and soul aligned,
In every moment, grace I find.

A compass true, my spirit sings,
In trusting You, my heart takes wings.
The journey's long, but I am whole,
With faith in You, I find my role.

Serenity's Sanctuary

Upon the hill where silence reigns,
In solace deep, the spirit gains.
A haven found, where shadows cease,
In sacred stillness, I find peace.

The gentle breeze, a hymn of praise,
In every leaf, Your love conveys.
Here in this sacred, holy space,
I feel the warmth of Your embrace.

With open heart, I breathe You in,
The world outside, a distant din.
In quiet moments, truth will bloom,
As light descends, dispelling gloom.

Where time stands still, I sense the call,
In prayerful whispers, I stand tall.
A sanctuary for the soul,
In Your sweet love, I am made whole.

In the Light of Forgiveness

In shadows cast by bitter tears,
I seek the light that calms my fears.
With open hands, I let it flow,
Forgiveness shines, a holy glow.

The weight I bore, too hard to keep,
In letting go, my spirit leaps.
Each moment claimed, a chance to mend,
In love's embrace, our lives transcend.

The broken past, a stepping stone,
In shared remorse, we're not alone.
With gentle words, we build anew,
In unity, our hearts break through.

From ashes rise, our souls alight,
In the glow of peace, we find our sight.
Together forged, a brighter way,
In the light of love, we choose to stay.

The Descent into Grace

In shadows deep, the light reveals,
A journey wrought with holy seals.
The spirit soars where angels glade,
Through trials faced, His love conveyed.

Upon the path, a whisper sings,
Of hope renewed, and joy it brings.
Each fallen tear, a seed of gold,
In grace's arms, the heart unfolds.

The dawn breaks forth with radiant rays,
Illuminating lost, dark ways.
In every step, His mercy flows,
A gentle hand, our hearts he chose.

In faith we find our footing sure,
His promises, forever pure.
With every breath, our souls we lift,
In grace's grace, we find our gift.

Let praises rise to Heaven's door,
In unity, we seek to soar.
For every soul, a sacred place,
In love divine, we find our grace.

Seraphic Visions of Renewal

From heights above, the vision streams,
Of radiant light, and holy dreams.
Awake, O heart, from slumber deep,
In sacred visions, truths we keep.

The wings of angels brush the skies,
With whispers soft that never die.
In every moment, they bestow,
The seeds of peace, a gentle flow.

In gardens lush, where spirits dance,
We find renewal, given chance.
With eyes of faith, the world's anew,
In every breath, His love shines through.

No chains can bind the soul that sings,
For in His light, our hearts take wings.
A symphony of grace unfolds,
In seraphic warmth, our hope beholds.

So let us gather, hearts aligned,
In unity, our dreams combined.
For every soul, a spark divine,
In seraphic visions, love will shine.

Mending the Frayed Ties

In tender moments, hearts may break,
Yet from the cracks, new bonds we make.
With gentle hands, we start to weave,
The tapestry of love, believe.

Each word a thread, each vow a stitch,
In sacred trust, we find our niche.
For every wound, a chance to heal,
In love's embrace, our souls are real.

Through trials faced, we rise anew,
With faith as anchor, strong and true.
In shadows cast, the light will gleam,
Restoring hope, igniting dream.

Forgiveness blooms where pain once grew,
A garden rich, with colors true.
As seasons change, we hold each other,
In every heart, a sacred mother.

Together we shall face the storm,
In unity, we find our form.
For love unites what once was frayed,
In mending hearts, our peace is laid.

Echoes of the Divine Touch

The breeze that carries whispers near,
Is filled with echoes, sweet and clear.
In every sigh, a prayer does rise,
A testament beneath the skies.

Each moment holds a sacred spark,
Of love entwined, where souls embark.
In quietude, we feel His grace,
In every heartbeat, find our place.

The stars reveal His guiding hand,
In cosmic dance, a grander plan.
With open hearts, we dare to trust,
In faith's embrace, we rise from dust.

As morning breaks, His light does shine,
Illuminating paths divine.
In every trial, joy takes flight,
Through echoes soft, we find the light.

So let us walk where angels tread,
Embracing love, where hope is bred.
For in our hearts, forever clutch,
The echoes of the Divine touch.

The Sacred Confluence of Hearts

In silence, we gather near,
Hearts entwined, whispers clear.
In the light of the dawn's embrace,
Love flows freely, a sacred space.

Together we rise, spirits soar,
Bonded by faith, forevermore.
In harmony, we sing our song,
Bound by truth, where we belong.

Through trials faced, we hold on tight,
Guided by the stars at night.
In every tear, a lesson learned,
In every flame, our passion burned.

With open arms, we seek the grace,
Divine whispers in time and place.
In unity, we find our way,
The sacred confluence leads the day.

So let us walk, hand in hand,
Together, we rise and stand.
In love's embrace, our spirits meet,
In every heartbeat, make us complete.

In the Wake of Reverence

In the stillness of the night,
We gather, hearts burning bright.
With every prayer, a gentle plea,
In the wake of reverence, we see.

Through shadows cast by earthly fear,
We find the light that draws us near.
In each heartbeat, faith ignites,
Through trials faced, we grasp the heights.

With humble minds and open eyes,
We seek the truth that never lies.
In silence, wisdom often speaks,
In every moment, love unique.

We spread our arms to welcome grace,
Embracing life in every space.
In unity, our spirits blend,
In the wake of reverence, we mend.

So let us tread this sacred path,
Banishing doubt, embracing faith.
In gratitude, our voices rise,
In the wake of reverence, we are wise.

Pathways of Grace

Through valleys low and mountains high,
We walk the pathways, you and I.
In every step, a story told,
In pathways of grace, we are bold.

With every breath, our spirits sing,
Embracing hope in everything.
Through storms we rise, unyielding and strong,
In love's embrace, where we belong.

In laughter shared and tears we weep,
We sow the seeds that we shall reap.
Through trials faced, we grow in grace,
In every moment, we find our place.

With open hearts, we seek the light,
In the darkness, we shine so bright.
Together we walk, hand in hand,
On pathways of grace, we understand.

So let us dance in faith's embrace,
Finding strength in every trace.
In this journey, love interlaces,
Creating ever new pathways of grace.

Steps in Sacred Light

Beneath the stars, our spirits climb,
In steps of sacred light, we rhyme.
With every heartbeat, energy flows,
In love's embrace, our essence glows.

With gentle whispers guiding our way,
We find the strength to face the day.
In harmony, we follow the call,
Each step taken, we rise and fall.

Through valleys deep and peaks so steep,
We carry dreams that run so deep.
In each encounter, wisdom shared,
In steps of sacred light, we dared.

As shadows fade, and dawn appears,
We walk in faith, releasing fears.
In unity, our spirits unite,
In each moment, steps in sacred light.

So let us journey, hand in hand,
In this grand, divine, sacred land.
With hearts ignited, we take our flight,
In every step, we find our light.

Chronicles of the Soul's Awakening

In silent whispers of the night,
The spirit stirs, begins to rise.
Faint echoes of divinity,
Awakening within the skies.

Each star a guide, a distant ray,
Leading hearts to sacred ground.
In the stillness of the soul,
True purpose can be found.

Through trials faced and valleys deep,
A journey fraught with light and dark.
The flame within begins to leap,
Igniting passion's sacred spark.

The soul ascends, transcends the pain,
With every breath, a new refrain.
Divine whispers teach the way,
In grace, we rise, our fears allayed.

Awake, arise, oh weary heart,
The dawn is here, a brand new start.
Embrace the light, let shadows fade,
In love's embrace, the path is laid.

Threads of Grace and Compassion

In every heart, compassion weaves,
A tapestry of love and grace.
With gentle hands, the spirit leaves,
Imprints of kindness in each place.

The thread of hope, a vibrant hue,
Stitches the wounds of sorrow's pain.
Through acts of love, we see anew,
Together, we rise, the heart's domain.

In every whispered prayer we share,
The fabric of our souls aligns.
With every gesture, every care,
The light of grace in love enshrines.

As rivers flow, compassion spreads,
Nurturing the weary soul.
From humble hearts, the Spirit leads,
In unity, we become whole.

Embrace the threads that bind us tight,
In harmony, we learn to shine.
With love as our eternal light,
Together, we create divine.

Rays of Redemption

From shadows cast, a light breaks through,
Illuminating paths we tread.
The dawn of grace, a promise new,
Whispers of hope where fears once led.

With every step, redemption calls,
A chorus born from ashes grey.
In faith, we rise, as the spirit falls,
Embracing love to guide the way.

The heart once heavy finds its song,
As sorrow melts beneath the sun.
Through trials faced, we grow more strong,
In every end, a new begun.

A balm for wounds, a gentle touch,
Forgiveness flows like rivers wide.
In every heart, we love so much,
With arms of light, we walk beside.

Redemption sings in every breath,
A melody of hope and grace.
In life's embrace, we conquer death,
In love's warm light, we find our place.

A Tapestry of Healing

In the fabric of existence,
Threads of love entwine and weave.
Healing whispers call us home,
In the peace that gently clings.

Through every tear, a lesson blooms,
A garden sown with seeds of grace.
In pain's embrace, the heart consumes,
The strength to rise in love's embrace.

As colors merge, the strokes align,
Our stories blend, each tale unique.
In unity, our hearts refine,
A masterpiece the soul will seek.

Each wound a note in healing's song,
Together we create the art.
With every breath, where we belong,
The tapestry of souls impart.

In quiet dawns and starry nights,
The threads of healing interlace.
Through life's embrace, in shared insights,
We find the light, divinity's grace.

Echoes of Serenity

In stillness, whispers rise,
Seeking grace from above,
Hearts entwined in silent prayer,
Embracing peace and love.

The soft glow of the dawn,
Guides our weary souls,
Paths of light laid before us,
As the spirit consoles.

Beneath the ancient trees,
Sacred truths do unfold,
Nature sings in harmony,
A promise pure and bold.

With every breath we take,
We find strength to endure,
In the echoes of serenity,
God's embrace is sure.

Through trials and tempests,
Hope remains steadfast,
The journey leads to wisdom,
In His love, we're cast.

A Covenant of Healing

In the quiet of the night,
Hands are clasped in prayer,
Heartfelt cries seek solace,
In this sacred air.

Breath of life, we gather,
Mending wounds unseen,
In faith, we find our refuge,
Like warm sunlight's beam.

Promises of tomorrow,
Nurtured in His grace,
Reviving weary spirits,
In this holy space.

With each gentle heartbeat,
Wisdom softly flows,
A covenant of healing,
Where love eternally grows.

Through trials we are tested,
In unity, we stand,
For peace is found in kindness,
A divine, healing hand.

Stones of Strength

In valleys deep and shadows long,
We find the stones of strength,
Carved by trials, shaped by faith,
Guiding us at length.

Each stone a story whispers,
Of battles fought and won,
Underneath the sunlit skies,
Our journey's just begun.

Together, we lift burdens,
And radiate His light,
In love's unwavering hands,
We rise to greater heights.

With every step we venture,
Our hearts forever bound,
In the faith that moves us onward,
In His grace, we are found.

So let us build a foundation,
On these stones of trust,
For with every step in prayer,
We grow, because we must.

The Altar of Reflection

Upon the altar of reflection,
We gather, hearts laid bare,
With gratitude, we soften,
In His presence, we share.

Each thought, a sacred offering,
In silence, souls unite,
The burdens heavy lifted,
In love's transcendent light.

We seek the path of goodness,
With every tear we've shed,
In surrender, we find freedom,
In the words unsaid.

The mirror of the spirit,
Reflects our deepest truth,
In vulnerability, we flourish,
Regaining youth through proof.

So let us stand in reverence,
With hearts forever free,
Embracing the altar of reflection,
Where we come to be.

Journeys to Resilience

In valleys low, we humbly tread,
With faith as guide, our hearts are fed.
Through storms that rage, we lift our gaze,
In every challenge, we find our praise.

Brick by brick, we build our core,
Each tear a lesson, each wound a door.
From ashes rise, we learn to stand,
Embracing hope with steady hands.

With whispered prayers, our fears subside,
In sacred trust, we turn the tide.
The path is long, but love will lead,
In every struggle, there lies a seed.

As dawn breaks forth, we find our way,
In unity, we fight the fray.
Together we rise, our spirits whole,
In every journey, we find our soul.

Pilgrimage of the Heart

With every step, we seek the light,
A journey sacred, day and night.
Through whispered winds, our prayers take flight,
In pilgrimage, we find what's right.

The heart's desires, a map divine,
In silence deep, our souls entwine.
With every tear, a story told,
In faith's embrace, we are consoled.

Mountains high, and valleys low,
We walk this path, where rivers flow.
In aching hearts, we hear the call,
Through love's sweet grace, we rise, we fall.

Each sacred moment, we hold dear,
In every heartbeat, love draws near.
With open arms, we face our fate,
In endless grace, we celebrate.

The Way of Renewal

Amidst the chaos, hope will bloom,
With every dawn, dispelling gloom.
In sacred rhythms, we find our voice,
To rise anew, in faith, rejoice.

The heart is mended by love's embrace,
In every trial, we find our place.
With gentle whispers from above,
We journey forth in grace and love.

The world around may start to fade,
But deep within, our light is made.
Through every moment, we find the way,
In every prayer, come what may.

Resilience grows in the soil of pain,
In every loss, there's much to gain.
Through storms we weather, we learn to dance,
In every heartbeat, there lies a chance.

Healing Through Faith

In shadows cast by doubt and fear,
We find the strength to persevere.
With every tear, we pave the way,
In faith's embrace, we learn to pray.

The spirit soars on wings of grace,
In every trial, we find our place.
Through sacred vows, our hearts unite,
In healing's light, we shine so bright.

Each story woven with threads of love,
In whispered prayers sent high above.
With every heartbeat, hope ignites,
In troubled times, our faith unites.

Through valleys deep, we rise again,
In every struggle, the strength of kin.
Together we stand, no longer alone,
In every journey, we've found our home.

Dawn of the Soul's Revival

In silence the spirit stirs anew,
Awakening light in shadows of strife.
The golden rays break through the gray,
A promise of hope in the journey of life.

With gentle breaths, the heart finds peace,
In whispers of grace that softly tread.
Each moment a gift, a chance to rise,
To dance in the light where doubts have fled.

Embrace the dawn, let shadows fade,
In the stillness, the soul shall sing.
A warm embrace of the morning glow,
Reviving dreams on angel's wings.

The past a lesson, the future bright,
In the love of the One, we find our way.
With faith as our guide, we take each step,
Walking in light, not led astray.

So let your spirit soar like a dove,
In the dawn of revival, find your song.
For in the depths of the sacred heart,
Resurrection blooms, where we belong.

The Sacred Pilgrimage

On the road less traveled lies the path,
Where seekers walk with fervent prayer.
Each step a testament to faith's embrace,
In the quiet, we find the divine there.

With every stone that we pass by,
Stories are woven in the dust of time.
The echoes of ancients guide our way,
In the sacred pilgrimage, life's own rhyme.

Mountains loom; the valleys call,
In the trials our spirits ignite.
For every stumble, a lesson learned,
Through shadows we step into the light.

Together we journey, hand in hand,
In fellowship, our burdens shared.
With hearts open wide, we breathe in grace,
In the sacredness of love declared.

So let us walk, with hope ablaze,
To the horizon where the sun greets night.
In the sacred pilgrimage of the spirit,
We find the dawn, we find our light.

Blossoms of Resilience

In the garden of trials, we take root,
Amidst the storms our spirits grow.
Each petal whispers a tale of strength,
Resilience blooms where the heart can glow.

Though thorns may prick, we stand tall,
With faith as the sun upon our face.
In every struggle, we find our voice,
A symphony of hope in sacred space.

As seasons change, the flowers rise,
Through winters cold, we learn to thrive.
For in the darkest nights of the soul,
Emerging light keeps our dreams alive.

Let compassion be the rain that falls,
Nourishing hearts with kindness so pure.
In the garden of life, let us make peace,
For blossoms of resilience ever endure.

So gather your strength, and hold on tight,
In unity, we find the power to heal.
With love as our seed, we cherish the fight,
Together we bloom, with spirits ideal.

Embracing the Brokenness

In the cracks of our hearts, light seeps through,
A mosaic of stories, both scarred and bright.
Each fracture a testament of love's embrace,
In brokenness lies the path to the light.

With open arms, we welcome the pain,
As the cloak of sorrow wraps us tight.
For in our wounds, grace finds a way,
Transforming our trials into radiant light.

The world may judge, but we see the truth,
In the beauty of scars, our strength reveals.
Embracing the broken, we rise from despair,
Finding the love in what life conceals.

So gather your pieces, don't hide away,
In vulnerability, we discover our song.
With unity in heart, let us stand as one,
Embracing the broken, we grow ever strong.

For in each fragile moment, hope does bloom,
An anthem of healing that swells the heart.
Through love and forgiveness, we shall unite,
Embracing the brokenness, a brand new start.

Healing Waters

In the quiet of dawn's embrace,
Flow the waters from grace's source,
Washing away the wounds of time,
Bringing peace to the weary heart.

Gentle ripples of sacred truth,
Whisper soft to the fragile soul,
Drink deeply of this holy light,
Find solace in the river's flow.

Beneath the surface, life transforms,
Colors bloom in the soul's expanse,
Restorative love in every drop,
A promise made, our spirits soar.

Let the current guide our steps,
While faith sustains our fragile will,
Miracles born within our reach,
As healing waters calm the storm.

With open hearts, we gather round,
The sacred stream of life divine,
Be refreshed, uplifted by grace,
In unity, forever thrive.

Beyond the Valley of Tears

In shadows deep, we tread the path,
Where sorrow whispers, shadows loom,
Yet faith ignites the hopeful flame,
Guiding hearts beyond the gloom.

Each tear a testament of strength,
A river flowing towards the light,
In loss, we find the threads of love,
Binding souls to reach new heights.

The mountains rise, the sun will shine,
Through every trial, we will grow,
With open arms, we welcome grace,
And trust the way we're meant to go.

Together on this sacred journey,
Hand in hand, we'll face the fight,
For beyond the valley's sorrow,
Awaits a world bathed in light.

Take heart, for joy breaks through the night,
Hope will bloom in the darkest hour,
Beyond the valley, life awaits,
A garden filled with heaven's power.

Miracles Along the Path

With every step, a chance to see,
The sacred woven through our days,
In the laughter of a child's play,
Miracles dance, in wondrous ways.

Where flowers bloom beneath the sun,
And hope is scattered like the seeds,
Each moment whispers of the one,
Who meets our heart with tender needs.

Beneath the stars, our dreams take flight,
In shared stories, bonds are forged,
The light of faith will guide us home,
As we walk the path we've carved.

In gentle breezes, hear the call,
Of love that surrounds, unconfined,
A tapestry of miracles,
Each thread a blessing intertwined.

So let us walk with heads held high,
Through valleys low and peaks so grand,
For miracles await our gaze,
Along this journey, hand in hand.

The Soul's Pilgrimage

Upon the road of faith we tread,
With every step, a prayer we raise,
In humble hearts, our spirits soar,
As we set forth to seek His ways.

With burdens born and dreams alive,
We journey through the trials of life,
Our souls ignited, searching wide,
For truth that cuts through earthly strife.

Amidst the shadows, light will break,
As morning dawns with softest touch,
Through valleys deep and mountains high,
Our hearts are called to love so much.

In fellowship, we find our strength,
Supporting one another's fight,
For every soul that seeks the path,
Shall find the road that leads to light.

Embrace the journey, fear not the way,
For grace will guide the steps we take,
Our pilgrimage a sacred quest,
To draw us close, our hearts awake.

Solace in the Struggle

In the darkness, prayers arise,
Hearts entwined in hope's embrace.
Through the trials, our spirits soar,
With faith that time cannot erase.

When shadows loom, and doubts appear,
We find our strength in love's sweet light.
Guided by the hand of grace,
We walk together through the night.

Every tear a sacred stream,
Each burden shared becomes a song.
In the struggle, we shall dream,
Bound by courage, we grow strong.

Though weary winds may howl and sway,
In unity, we shall not break.
With every step, we find our way,
Through trust, our soul's true path we make.

Let our burdens be laid down,
As we stand on sacred ground.
In the solace found in strife,
We grasp the gift of sacred life.

Echoes of Mercy

In the silence, whispers flow,
Gentle words that heal the soul.
Echoes of mercy softly glow,
Reminders that we are made whole.

Through every heart that seeks to mend,
Compassion's light will always shine.
In each embrace, we find a friend,
In every moment, love divine.

Gathered close in sacred space,
We share the burdens of our hearts.
Through the storm, we find our grace,
In unity, a brand new start.

Every hope that lifts us high,
Each prayer a beacon in the dark.
In the depths, our spirits fly,
Graced by love's eternal spark.

Let mercy flow like rivers wide,
Cleansing wounds and paving ways.
In the echoes, we confide,
With gratitude, our voices raise.

Radiance After the Storm

Dark clouds gather, winds may wail,
Yet within, a promise glows.
After the tempest, hope will prevail,
Like flowers through the earth that grows.

The sun will break through shaded skies,
With every dawn, a chance to rise.
From brokenness, a vision clear,
In the aftermath, God draws near.

With every shadow, light shall dance,
In trials, a sacred chance to see.
Through pain, we learn to take a stance,
Embracing love and unity.

As rainbows arch across the blue,
So too does beauty follow strife.
In every heart, a story true,
Of radiance that breathes new life.

Let not your spirit lose its flame,
For storms will pass, and still we stand.
In the quiet, love calls your name,
Embodying grace, hand in hand.

The Alchemy of Suffering

In the furnace, hearts are forged,
Suffering shapes the soul's design.
Through the fire, we are enlarged,
Turning pain into gems divine.

With every tear, we shed a weight,
In surrender, we find release.
Through trials faced, we cultivate,
The roots of deep and lasting peace.

In moments bleak, the light may fade,
Yet hope ignites in darkest night.
Our spirits free, though bruised and frayed,
We rise anew, embracing light.

For in each wound, a lesson clear,
Transformation whispers soft and low.
In the alchemy, we appear,
As vessels rich with love to show.

Let suffering guide, not confine,
In every trial, a chance to grow.
Through sacred alchemy, we find,
Strength to walk and heart to sow.

Rebirth in the Spirit

In shadows deep, where hope was lost,
A whisper stirs, revival's cost.
From ashes rise, the spirit gleams,
In grace bestowed, we chase our dreams.

Water flows, a sacred stream,
Nourishing hearts, igniting the beam.
With every breath, new life we claim,
Reborn in faith, we praise His name.

Through trials faced, we find our way,
In love's embrace, we learn to pray.
The heart reborn, a flame so bright,
Guiding us forth, into the light.

With open hands, we share the gift,
A tapestry of souls we lift.
In unity, our spirits bind,
In every heart, the truth we find.

Awake, arise, the dawn ignites,
In spirit's dance, we reach new heights.
With every step, our journey's clear,
Rebirth in spirit, we hold dear.

A Covenant of Healing

In brokenness, we seek the light,
A bond of love to mend our plight.
In whispered prayers, we find our way,
A covenant forged, a brighter day.

Through trials faced, our hearts align,
In kindness shared, our souls entwine.
With gentle hands, we heal the pain,
In unity, strength is gained.

Forgiveness flows, like rivers wide,
Together we stand, and none divide.
A sacred promise, forever true,
In faith and hope, we are made new.

With every tear, a lesson learned,
In love's embrace, our hearts have burned.
We rise anew, through grace unyielding,
In every moment, a spirit healing.

Bound by the light, we walk in peace,
In every breath, our doubts release.
A covenant strong, forever binds,
In healing hearts, our purpose finds.

The Promise of Dawn

When shadows fade with morning's grace,
New beginnings in every place.
With open hearts, we seek the way,
The promise bright, a brand new day.

From darkness deep, we rise as one,
In faith renewed, our journey's begun.
Each dawn a gift, with colors bold,
In every moment, stories unfold.

With whispered hopes, the future gleams,
In unity, we chase our dreams.
The sun breaks forth, a radiant sight,
Illuminating paths with light.

Together we stand, hands intertwined,
In love's embrace, the ties that bind.
Through trials faced, we find our way,
The promise of dawn, here to stay.

In every heartbeat, joy we find,
A sacred rhythm, hearts aligned.
With every dawn, the world awakes,
To love's sweet promise, the heart remakes.

Sacred Threads of Life

In woven light, our stories blend,
A tapestry of hearts, no end.
Each thread a life, unique and bright,
In sacred bonds, we share the light.

With tender care, we mend the seams,
In unity, we weave our dreams.
Through trials faced, and joys regained,
In love's embrace, the tapestry's stained.

From different paths, we come as one,
In harmony, the work's begun.
With every stitch, a purpose clear,
The sacred threads, forever near.

In laughter shared, and sorrow's song,
In every note, we all belong.
Together we rise, in faith's delight,
In sacred threads, we find our light.

With whispered hopes, our dreams take flight,
In every moment, day and night.
Bound by the grace of love's pure strife,
In sacred threads, we weave our life.

Hallowed Moments of Peace

In stillness, souls unite,
Beneath the vast and starry dome.
Whispers of grace, gentle light,
Embrace the heart, a timeless home.

In prayer, we gather strength,
Through faith, our spirits soar.
Each moment, a sacred length,
In love's embrace, forevermore.

The silence speaks of truth,
A path where every heart can roam.
In hallowed whispers of youth,
We find in God our holy tome.

With hope, we tread the vale,
In unity, we find our peace.
Through love's enduring trail,
Our fears and doubts shall cease.

Together in this blessed space,
We hear the call of heaven's grace.
With every breath, we touch the face,
Of all that time cannot erase.

The Art of Letting Go

In shadows cast by yesterday,
We learn to shed the heavy load.
In faith, we find a brighter way,
As grace unfolds along the road.

Each tear that falls, a seed of light,
Releasing pain, embracing hope.
In silence, we ignite the fight,
To rise anew, beyond the scope.

The chains of doubt begin to break,
As trust in God becomes our guide.
In letting go, our hearts awake,
To love that constantly abides.

Like autumn leaves that dance and play,
We find our freedom in the breeze.
In every step, our souls convey,
A testament of inner peace.

Embrace the ebb, the flow, the grace,
For every end brings such a start.
In every loss, we trace the face,
Of hope that blossoms in the heart.

The Light Beyond

In twilight's hush, a beacon glows,
A flame that lights the path we seek.
With every step, our spirit grows,
In search of solace for the weak.

Beyond the clouds, the heavens speak,
With whispers soft as morning dew.
In faith, the strong and tender meek,
Discover love that is so true.

The twilight fades, yet still it shines,
A promise held in sacred space.
Through trials faced, our heart aligns,
And life transforms by God's embrace.

Through every shadow, light will break,
A dance of grace, a sacred call.
In union, hearts begin to wake,
In hope, we rise, we shall not fall.

A tapestry of love divine,
In each heartbeat, we are reborn.
The light beyond does brightly shine,
A testament to each new morn.

Divine Tides of Healing

In waves of mercy, grace descends,
A sacred flow that binds us all.
With every rise, true love transcends,
In gentle whispers, we hear the call.

Through trials faced upon this shore,
The tides of hope restore the soul.
In letting go, we are made more,
Each broken piece, a part made whole.

In solace found in nature's song,
We gather strength within the storm.
In unity, we grow more strong,
Through every tear, existence warms.

Washing over with radiant grace,
God's hand paints the path anew.
In every trial, love's embrace,
Heals wounds that time and fear construe.

So let us dance upon the shore,
Beneath the heavens, bright and wide.
In divine tides, forevermore,
We find our peace, our loving guide.

Lanterns on Dusk's Path

Beneath the starry sky's embrace,
The lanterns guide our way with grace.
Through shadows deep and whispers slight,
We seek the path to sacred light.

In every heart, a flame does stir,
Illuminating hope's soft blur.
Each step we take, a prayer we share,
In unity, we rise from despair.

The dusk may fall, but faith will rise,
Like morning sun that paints the skies.
With every struggle, every sigh,
We find our strength; we learn to fly.

So let the lanterns shine so bright,
Guiding souls through the endless night.
Together in the love we seek,
We'll find the peace that makes us whole.

Embracing the Journey Within

In silence deep, the heart will find,
A journey rich, where souls unwind.
With every breath, a step we take,
Into the depths, for wisdom's sake.

Embrace the whispers, still and clear,
Unravel doubts, confront your fear.
The path to self unveils the grace,
That blooms within our sacred space.

As rivers flow and seasons change,
Our spirits grow, our lives arrange.
In tender moments, truth appears,
Transforming pain into our fears.

Through trials faced, we come to know,
The strength within, the seeds we sow.
With every heartbeat, love's embrace,
Guides us home to our sacred place.

The Healing Embrace of Silence

In quietude, we find our peace,
A balm for wounds that never cease.
Within the stillness, echoes fade,
And hope emerges, unafraid.

The noise of life can drown the soul,
Yet silence makes the broken whole.
A refuge found in whispered prayers,
Where every heartache gently bears.

Embrace the hush, let spirit soar,
In sacred space, we conquer war.
With every sigh, the burdens lift,
In gentle release, we find our gift.

So rest awhile in silence pure,
For in this stillness, we endure.
The healing touch of calm surrounds,
In silence deep, our hope abounds.

Veils of Suffering

Beneath the veils where shadows dwell,
The stories woven, hearts compel.
In every tear, a tale unfolds,
Of trials faced, of courage bold.

Yet in the dark, the light shines through,
The strength within begins to brew.
From suffering, our spirits rise,
Transforming pain into our skies.

These veils of grief, they drift away,
Revealing hope in light of day.
With every breath, let love be known,
In wounds and scars, we find our home.

So walk with grace through trials vast,
Embrace the lessons that will last.
For in each struggle, there is light,
A promise whispered, 'You will fight.'

Sacred Footprints

In silence, we tread on sacred ground,
Each step a whisper, where love is found.
Hearts uplifted, souls entwined,
In every footprint, grace aligned.

The path of light, a guiding thread,
With faith we walk, where angels tread.
Through trials faced, and burdens shared,
In sacred footprints, we are spared.

The earth reflects a holy glow,
A journey marked by all we sow.
In every stride, a prayer ascends,
With hope each heart, the spirit mends.

Through valleys low and mountains high,
In sacred footprints, spirits fly.
Together we march, a blessed throng,
In unity, we find where we belong.

The path unfolds with lessons clear,
In every trial, the truth draws near.
With love as our guide, we shall arise,
In sacred footprints, we touch the skies.

The Divine Ascent

Upward we climb, with hearts aflame,
In search of truth, we call His name.
Each step we take, a sacred vow,
To seek the light in the here and now.

The mountain's peak, a place divine,
With every breath, our spirits shine.
The path may narrow, but faith endures,
In the Divine Ascent, our heart is sure.

Through clouds of doubt and shadows deep,
We rise above, our souls to keep.
For in the struggle, we find our grace,
The Divine Ascent, our sacred space.

With open hands, we let love flow,
Each offering made, helping us grow.
In unity, our voices blend,
The call of the Divine, our journey's end.

At journey's close, we look with pride,
For in each challenge, faith was our guide.
The Divine Ascent, our spirits soar,
In love eternal, forevermore.

Through Shadows to Sunlight

Through shadows cast, we walk with grace,
With faith as our shield, we find our place.
In the darkest hour, hope still gleams,
Guiding our hearts, igniting dreams.

When wearied souls begin to break,
In silent prayer, we find the strength.
Through shadows deep, the light draws near,
In faith's embrace, we find no fear.

The dawn shall rise, with colors bright,
Through shadows past, we seek the light.
With every step, the heart learns trust,
In the journey onward, we must adjust.

Each shadow fades, revealing grace,
With hands held high, we seek His face.
Through prayers whispered, to skies above,
We find our way, led by love.

Through shadows soft, into the day,
With light reborn, we find our way.
In gratitude for every trial,
Through shadows to sunlight, we walk the aisle.

Blessings on the Journey

Each blessing gathered like morning dew,
A gift of hope, forever true.
In every mile, the heart is stirred,
Through whispered prayers, our voices heard.

With open hearts we face the day,
Blessings on the journey guide our way.
Through valleys low and mountains grand,
Stronger together, hand in hand.

The road may twist, the night may fall,
Yet love prevails and answers the call.
In each embrace, we share our light,
Blessings on the journey, our guiding sight.

With faith as our compass, we forge ahead,
For every tear, a joy to spread.
Through trials faced and dreams attained,
Blessings on the journey forever remain.

In unity, we rise above,
With open arms and endless love.
Embracing all, we take our stance,
Blessings on the journey, our sacred dance.

Refuge in the Sacred Silence

In the stillness, I find my peace,
A gentle whisper, my fears release.
The world fades into soft refrain,
In sacred silence, I break my chain.

Each breath a prayer, each moment divine,
In the quiet, I draw the line.
The heart speaks truth, when others won't hear,
In this refuge, I cast aside fear.

The light within softly begins to glow,
Guiding my spirit, teaching me to flow.
With every heartbeat, wisdom unwinds,
In the silence, my soul entwines.

I walk the path of the purest grace,
Finding reflection in every face.
In the embrace of stillness, I stand,
United in love, hand in hand.

In sacred silence, the world transforms,
A symphony of spirit that calmly performs.
With faith as my anchor, I rise, uplifted,
In this refuge, my heart is gifted.

The Altar of Change

At the altar of change, I kneel and pray,
Seeking guidance for each passing day.
With open heart, I release the past,
Embracing the future, my shadows cast.

In the flames of renewal, I find my truth,
The wisdom of ages, the essence of youth.
With every challenge, a chance to grow,
In the dance of life, I trust and flow.

The whispers of movement, a sacred song,
Calling me onward, where I belong.
In surrender, I find my strength anew,
In the altar of change, I trust what is true.

With each heartbeat, transformation ignites,
Navigating the darkness, embracing the lights.
Every moment a gift, every breath a sign,
At the altar of change, the divine aligns.

In the journey ahead, I embrace the unknown,
For within every trial, my spirit has grown.
In the warmth of transition, I learn to believe,
At the altar of change, I freely receive.

Whispers of Grace

In the gentle breeze, I hear a call,
Whispers of grace that touch us all.
Like petals falling, soft and light,
They guide my steps in the darkest night.

Each moment bestowed, a blessing in time,
Filled with promise, in rhythm and rhyme.
The echoes of love, through valleys they trace,
Reminding me always of infinite grace.

Through trials faced, I hear the song,
A melody sweet, where I belong.
In the heart's embrace, the spirit takes flight,
With whispers of grace, I walk in light.

In the quiet of being, I find the way,
Each step a canvas, painted each day.
The laughter of angels, the tears that we shed,
In whispers of grace, my spirit is fed.

As the dawn breaks anew, hope starts to rise,
In the dance of existence, I reach for the skies.
With every breath, I let love efface,
In the sacred journey, I claim my place.

Constellations of Healing

In the night sky, a tapestry glows,
Constellations of healing, the wisdom flows.
Each star a story, each light a guide,
In the cosmos of love, my sorrows subside.

The universe whispers in colors so bright,
Shadows of struggle illuminated by light.
In the dance of the planets, I find my peace,
With every alignment, my heart finds release.

Through the lens of the heavens, I see the way,
The journey unfolds with each passing day.
In the vastness of all, I hear the call,
Constellations of healing embrace us all.

In the stillness of night, I hold the stars near,
Their wisdom is timeless, their presence is clear.
In the spaces in between, I learn to forgive,
For in each constellation, we learn how to live.

As we gather in wonder, hearts open wide,
With gratitude flowing, in love we abide.
Constellations of healing, a beacon of grace,
In the universe's embrace, we each find our place.

Beneath the Weight of Wounds

In the silence of the night, prayers ascend,
Each whispered hope, a message to the end.
Beneath the weight of wounds we carry deep,
Faith is the promise, the light we keep.

When shadows stretch and doubts arise,
The heart finds strength, the spirit flies.
In every tear, a lesson unfolds,
In every sorrow, a story told.

The burdens we bear are not ours alone,
In togetherness, the seeds are sown.
Through trials faced, we learn to trust,
In grace and mercy, we rise from dust.

With every struggle, a bond is made,
In faith and love, our fears do fade.
For in the wounds, the healing starts,
A testament to the brave of hearts.

And so we walk this path of pain,
Embracing storms, through sun and rain.
For in each struggle, strength anew,
Beneath the weight, Christ walks with you.

Illumination Through Struggle

In darkest hours, the soul shall shine,
For trials come to mold your spine.
Each test, a step toward the divine,
Illumination through struggle, a sacred sign.

When tempests rage and voices shout,
In quiet moments, cast away doubt.
For in the fire, the gold is found,
In hardships faced, His love abounds.

Through every trial, our faith grows clear,
The whispers of hope, the whispers we hear.
With every burden, a lesson learned,
In paths of chaos, the heart has turned.

As mountains loom and rivers swell,
In courage, we find our sacred well.
Through shadows cast, His light breaks through,
Illumination in all we pursue.

In every struggle, we rise anew,
He leads us on, faithful and true.
With hearts aflame, our spirits soar,
Through illumination, we find our core.

The Dawn of Understanding

As shadows fade with morning's light,
The dawn of understanding, pure and bright.
In gentle whispers, the truth is laid,
With open hearts, our fears allayed.

In every question, a journey starts,
In seeking answers, we grow smart.
With each new dawn, the spirit wakes,
In paths of love, the heart re-takes.

Through trials faced, the lessons clear,
The voice of wisdom drawing near.
In moments still, the answers flow,
The dawn reveals what we must know.

With every heartbeat, we learn to see,
The love of God, eternally free.
In every sunrise, a promise made,
The dawn of understanding, never fade.

With open minds, we rise in grace,
In every trial, we find our place.
For in the light, the truth expands,
The dawn of understanding, in His hands.

Heavenly Sojourn

In every step, a journey unfolds,
A heavenly sojourn, the heart beholds.
With each new dawn, the path is clear,
In faith we walk, without fear.

Through valleys deep and mountains high,
With wings of love, we soar the sky.
In laughter shared and tears embraced,
A celestial journey, our souls are chaste.

Through trials faced, the spirit grows,
In every challenge, our purpose knows.
With grace, we find the strength to rise,
A heavenly sojourn, the soul's prize.

In unity, we find our song,
A melody of faith, for we belong.
The path is winding, yet we stay true,
In heavenly sojourn, life anew.

For every moment, a treasure bright,
In every heart, the divine light.
So hand in hand, we walk on through,
A heavenly sojourn, me and you.

Paths of Restoration

In the valley, whispers call,
Hearts beat gently, one and all.
Hope arises, clouds depart,
Faith, the healing of the heart.

With every step, a promise true,
Guided by the light in you.
Each misstep leads to grace,
Restoration in His embrace.

Through trials faced and shadows cast,
Joy arrives, the storms won't last.
Mercy flows, a river wide,
In the stillness, we abide.

Surrender doubts, let love unfold,
In His warmth, let courage hold.
Paths of peace, through trials steep,
Trust in Him, your soul's to keep.

So journey forth, beloved child,
In the quiet, grow more wild.
Spirit whispers, softly speak,
Paths of Restoration seek.

Grace in the Wilderness

In the desert, where hearts roam,
Grace, the ever-present home.
In the stillness, find your breath,
Life renewed beyond all death.

Winds will carry prayers to God,
Step by step upon this sod.
Every thorn, a lesson learned,
In the fire, your heart is burned.

Look around, the beauty glows,
In the hardships, wisdom grows.
Every moment, softly flows,
Grace in wilderness, it shows.

Trust the path, though steep it be,
In His hands, you'll always see.
Through the struggles, find the way,
Grace, the light that never sways.

In the night, His stars will shine,
Guiding souls to love divine.
Wilderness teaches, faith is key,
Grace, our guide eternally.

The Light Beyond Shadows

In the darkness, hope retreats,
Yet the heart still softly beats.
Shadows whisper lies of fear,
But the truth is always near.

With every prayer, a spark ignites,
In the depth of darkest nights.
Faith shall carve a path anew,
The light beyond is calling you.

See the dawn break through the night,
Warm embrace, the sacred light.
Every tear a seed of grace,
Blooming in a holy space.

Lift your gaze, and you shall find,
In His love, the ties that bind.
Through the trials, walk in trust,
For in Him, we rise from dust.

Shadows fade when hearts believe,
In His promise, we receive.
The light shines bright, a guiding hand,
Leading to the promised land.

Sanctum of the Heart

Within the stillness of the soul,
Lies a love that makes us whole.
Sanctum pure, a sacred space,
Where we find our Father's grace.

In the quiet, listen near,
Every whisper, holds Him dear.
Seek the truth, let worries cease,
In this haven, dwell in peace.

Joy and sorrow, hand in hand,
In His love, we understand.
Hearts united, never part,
In the sanctum, truth impart.

Let the burdens melt away,
In His presence, here we stay.
In the glow of love's embrace,
Sanctum of the heart, our place.

Reach for hope, and hold it tight,
Guided always by His light.
Within our hearts, the treasure lives,
Sanctum pure, where love forgives.

The Divine Embrace of Change

In shadows deep, the light we seek,
Through trials faced, we hear Him speak.
A gentle shift, the winds do call,
In change, we rise, in love, we fall.

Embrace the storm, let spirits soar,
For every door, He opens more.
Roots growing strong, in faith we stand,
The Creator guides with tender hand.

With every dawn, a promise bright,
Unraveling dreams, revealing light.
Each step we take, His grace unfolds,
Transforming hearts, as stories told.

In sacred whispers, truths revealed,
The pain we've borne, now gently healed.
Embrace the change, with open heart,
In love's pure flow, we play our part.

Steps of Faith

With every step, the path unfolds,
His whispers guide, as truth beholds.
In moments fraught with doubt and fear,
A steadfast heart, the way draws near.

Through shadows thick, our faith ignites,
With every prayer, we find new heights.
The promises etched on our souls,
In quiet trust, we find our roles.

Together we walk, hand in hand,
In faith's embrace, united we stand.
Each challenge faced, a lesson learned,
With hearts ablaze, our spirits turned.

In paths unknown, we still shall roam,
For in His arms, we find our home.
With every beat, our hearts proclaim,
In steps of faith, we share His name.

Healing in Community

In circles drawn, we gather near,
Our hearts united, hopes sincere.
Each story shared, a balm for pain,
In love's embrace, we break each chain.

With hands held tight, we lift each soul,
Together mending, we become whole.
In laughter's echoes and tears we share,
The healing light, a bond so rare.

In kindness given, compassion seen,
We serve each other, and hearts convene.
With grace bestowed, our burdens light,
In community's strength, we find our might.

Through trials faced and joys expressed,
In unity, our hearts confessed.
To love each other is our creed,
In healing's touch, our spirits freed.

The Garden of Hope

In gardens lush, where flowers bloom,
A refuge found from life's great gloom.
With tender care, each seed we sow,
In rich embrace, let faith then grow.

Among the thorns, the beauty shines,
In every heart, His love aligns.
With water pure, our spirits thrive,
In hopeful light, we come alive.

The sun will rise, dispelling dread,
In every tear, He gently led.
With open eyes, we see the grace,
In every moment, find His face.

Through seasons change, our roots hold fast,
In garden's grace, we grow at last.
A tapestry of hope, we weave,
In sacred soil, we learn to believe.

Wings of Redemption

Through valleys deep, where shadows play,
A light emerges, guiding the way.
Forgiveness flows like a river wide,
On wings of hope, we rise and glide.

In whispered prayers, our burdens cease,
With every heartbeat, we find our peace.
The past releases its heavy chains,
In love's embrace, our spirit gains.

Beneath the stars, we seek the truth,
In faith renewed, we find our youth.
Together we soar, hand in hand,
With hearts ablaze, we take a stand.

The journey long, but souls entwined,
In sacred moments, love is defined.
Each step we take, a sacred vow,
With wings of redemption, we rise now.

Glimmers of Grace

In twilight's glow, where silence sings,
A spark ignites, and hope takes wings.
Through trials faced, our spirits shine,
In glimmers of grace, we intertwine.

With open hearts, we share the light,
Dispelling shadows, bringing sight.
In every sorrow, joy is found,
In love's embrace, we're heaven-bound.

The world may change, but truth remains,
In acts of kindness, love sustains.
With grateful hearts, we sing and pray,
In glimmers of grace, we find our way.

Together, we rise, hand in hand,
In unity's strength, we make our stand.
The beauty of life, a sacred trace,
In every moment, glimmers of grace.

The Harmony of Acceptance

In quiet moments, our hearts unfold,
In the dance of life, our stories told.
With gentle whispers, we learn to see,
The harmony found in you and me.

Each voice unique, a sacred song,
In unity's chorus, we all belong.
With open arms, we gather near,
In acceptance, love conquers fear.

Through stormy seas, we hold the course,
In faith and trust, we draw our force.
In every trial, a lesson learned,
In the warmth of love, our hearts have turned.

Together we walk, on this sacred ground,
With every heartbeat, a love profound.
In the tapestry woven, light shines bright,
The harmony of acceptance ignites.

Sanctum of the Soul

In sacred spaces where silence dwells,
The whispers of spirit, their stories tell.
With every breath, we seek the whole,
In the gentle sanctum of the soul.

With hands uplifted, we call on grace,
In the depths of night, we find our place.
In meditation's peace, we come alive,
In sacred stillness, our hearts thrive.

Through trials faced, we rise above,
In every moment, we feel the love.
With every heartbeat, we are made whole,
In the eternal sanctum of the soul.

Together we dwell, our spirits aligned,
In this sacred journey, our hearts intertwined.
With gratitude shining, we find our goal,
In the sanctuary deep within the soul.

Guided by Love

In the warmth of the light above,
Our hearts find peace, we rise and shove.
With each step that we take in grace,
Love leads us to our rightful place.

Through trials and storms, we seek the way,
With faith as our compass, we shall not stray.
In sacred bond, we walk as one,
Bound by the love of the Holy Son.

Mountains high and valleys low,
Together in spirit, we shall grow.
In each soul's embrace, a gentle touch,
United in love, we seek so much.

With hearts ablaze, and voices raised,
We sing the truth, our spirits praised.
In love's pure light, we now believe,
Guided by love, we shall achieve.

So let us shine, a beacon bright,
Reflecting love in the darkest night.
For in our unity, we find our way,
Guided by love, come what may.

Restoration of the Spirit

From ashes rise, our spirits flee,
Towards the dawn, in hope we see.
With lifted hands, we seek the grace,
Restoration found in His embrace.

In moments lost, we feel the pain,
Yet through the storm, our faith remains.
With gentle whispers, His love ignites,
Our hearts restored, reclaiming light.

The barren ground now blooms anew,
Faithful hearts, in praise we strew.
With every breath, we feel His near,
Restore our spirit, calm our fear.

In trials faced, we find the call,
To rise again, to stand, not fall.
With every heartbeat, His voice we hear,
Restoration comes, our path is clear.

So let the spirit soar up high,
On wings of love, we'll touch the sky.
For in the restoration of our soul,
We find the light that makes us whole.

Hallowed Echoes of Hope

In the stillness of the night,
Whispers of hope, a guiding light.
Echoes linger in the air,
Reminding us that Love is there.

Through shadows cast by doubt and fear,
The solace found brings us near.
With every breath, let faith arise,
In hallowed echoes, our spirits rise.

For every tear that marks the past,
We find the strength, our souls steadfast.
In hope we trust, with hearts entwined,
The promise of love, in spirit aligned.

In moments spent in quiet prayer,
Hallowed echoes fill the air.
With open hearts, we lift our song,
In hope enduring, we will belong.

So let us gather, hand in hand,
United in hope, a faithful band.
Together we'll walk, through trials cope,
With hallowed echoes, we find our hope.

The Sacred Whisper Within

In quiet moments, voices call,
The sacred whisper touches all.
Deep within, where love abides,
A gentle force that guides and guides.

In silence found, we pause, we pray,
Seeking truth in every way.
With hearts attuned to God's own song,
The sacred whisper calls us strong.

Through doubt's embrace, we hear the sound,
Of love's sweet grace all around.
With faith renewed, we realize,
The sacred truth with open eyes.

In every trial, in every fight,
The whisper soft ignites the light.
With courage bold, we face the day,
The sacred whisper shows the way.

So listen close, let spirits soar,
For in our hearts, there's something more.
The sacred whisper, pure and true,
Brings forth the light, forever new.

Embracing the Stillness

In the quiet of morning, a whisper calls,
Peace descends softly, where the heart enthralls.
In stillness, we find grace, a sacred soft glow,
Guided by faith, in the silence we grow.

Each breath a communion, each thought a prayer,
In the hush of the moment, His presence is there.
Waves of distraction, like shadows may fall,
But here in the stillness, I surrender it all.

Time holds its breath, while the spirit takes flight,
In the depths of the silence, I dance with the light.
A refuge of solace, a divine embrace,
Here I am anchored, in this holy space.

The hush speaks in language beyond what is known,
In deep contemplation, I feel not alone.
Miracles blossom in the calm of the heart,
In the stillness, the world plays a beautiful part.

In embracing this stillness, my spirit shall rise,
Finding strength in surrender, a love that belies.
Cloaked in the quiet, I witness His might,
In every soft heartbeat, His grace is the light.

Wellspring of Mercy

From the depths of the soul, a river does flow,
A wellspring of mercy, a love that will grow.
Each drop a reminder of grace ever true,
In the arms of compassion, I'm made fresh and new.

When shadows encircle, and hearts come undone,
This wellspring of mercy shines bright like the sun.
It heals all the wounds that the world leaves behind,
In the depths of His love, true solace I find.

An ocean of kindness, vast and profound,
In the embrace of His mercy, true peace can be found.
Though storms may surround, and trials may rage,
I drink from the well of His love on each page.

The gift of forgiveness flows freely to all,
In its gentle embrace, I find strength to stand tall.
For every transgression, His mercy provides,
A wellspring of hope that eternally guides.

In moments of doubt, when I lose my way,
This wellspring of mercy brightens the day.
With each step I take, I commit to His grace,
In the heart of His love, I've found my true place.

Transcending the Trials

Through storms that rage fiercely and winds that might howl,
I find in the struggle, a quiet, strong prowl.
Each trial a teacher, with lessons to share,
In the fire of passion, I learn how to care.

With faith as my compass, I rise from the dust,
Transcending the trials, in the Lord I trust.
Every tear that I shed is a step toward the light,
In darkness, His presence turns wrong into right.

The mountains may tremble, the valleys may bend,
But through each challenge, my spirit ascends.
In the arms of His love, I'm held ever tight,
Each trial an arrow, shot forth from His might.

A journey of courage, of growth, and of grace,
In the heart of my struggle, I seek to embrace.
For every heartache, there's wisdom I gain,
Transcending the trials, I'm free from the chains.

So let the winds blow, let the waves crash high,
With faith as my anchor, I'll reach for the sky.
For beyond every trial, there's a purpose divine,
In the story of struggle, His light will always shine.

Revelations in Suffering

In the depths of my sorrow, revelations unfold,
Through pain's bitter journey, new stories are told.
In shadows I wander, yet find light within,
For every dark moment, His love shall begin.

Each tear that I shed is a sacred release,
In the heart of the struggle, I find sweet peace.
Through trials I witness the strength of the soul,
In suffering's grasp, I am made ever whole.

The anguish may linger, but a purpose comes clear,
In the midst of the suffering, I know He is near.
Lessons emerge like the dawn's gentle ray,
Revelations of love, pushing darkness away.

When burdens feel heavy, and hope seems so far,
I search for His embrace, my guiding North Star.
In the pain of existence, I come to understand,
The depth of His mercy held gently in hand.

With each revelation, I rise from the fall,
Finding beauty in trials, His grace after all.
For in suffering's arms, great blessings will flow,
Revelations in heartache, His love starts to glow.

Milton Keynes UK
Ingram Content Group UK Ltd.
UKHW020039271124
451585UK00012B/944